WESTERN SOCIETY OF
MALACOLOGISTS

FIELD GUIDE

to the

SLUG

David George Gordon

SASQUATCH BOOKS
SEATTLE

Printed in the United States of America

Cover design and illustration: Dugald Stermer
Back cover photo: European black slug (*Arion ater*), by Dennis Paulson
Text illustrations: Joyce Bergen
Composition: grafX

Library of Congress Cataloging in Publication Data

Gordon, David G. (David George), 1950–
    Field guide to the slug / David George Gordon.
        p. cm.—(Sasquatch field guide series)
    At head of title: Western Society of Malacologists.
    Includes bibliographical references.
    ISBN 1-57061-011-8 : $5.95
    1. Slugs (Mollusks) 2. Slugs (Mollusks)—Control.
    I. Western Society of Malacologists. II. Title. III. Series.
QL430.4.G65 1994   94-6479
594'.3—dc20   CIP

Sasquatch Books
1008 Western Avenue
Seattle, Washington 98104
(206)467-4300

Other titles in the Sasquatch Field Guide series:

The Audubon Society
Field Guide to the Bald Eagle

The Oceanic Society
Field Guide to the Gray Whale

American Cetacean Society
Field Guide to the Orca

International Society of Cryptozoology
Field Guide to the Sasquatch

Great Bear Foundation
Field Guide to the Grizzly Bear

Adopt-a-Stream Foundation
Field Guide to the Pacific Salmon

Oceanic Society Expeditions/Earthtrust
Field Guide to the Humpback Whale

Contents

Introduction

I would be the first to admit that slugs are as repulsive as they are fascinating to people. After all, these animals smell with their bodies, come equipped with more teeth than a shark, and can glide without difficulty over broken glass, propelled by the rhythmic contractions of a single muscular foot. Their blood is green, and while other animals wrap themselves in fur, feathers, or scales, a slug protects its body with an all-encompassing layer of slime.

However, I am also obliged to stand up for slugs. In general, they've been given a bum rap by gardeners, who regularly battle the many nonnative slug species accidentally introduced to the Pacific Northwest from Europe and Asia. People tend to overlook the contributions of Northwest native slug species— perhaps not in our gardens but certainly in the wild, where they help disperse seeds and spores, break down decaying plant matter, and quite possibly keep other populations of small pests in check. Believe me, we would miss slugs should we somehow eliminate them from our forests and fields.

Throughout the Northwest, slugs have been cast as mascots of the bizarre (although that may be an upgrade of sorts for these much maligned creatures). I purchased my first piece of slugabilia, a bright red T-shirt with the silk-screened slogan "Slugs of Mystery," at Seattle's Pike Place Market in 1981. Since then, I've seen numerous slug-related novelties: color postcards, kitchen magnets, woodcarvings, candies, even cans of "Manhattan-Style Slug Chowder" (or so said a label pasted over the orginal). It is my hope that one day the demand for these items will exceed that of poison-laden slug and snail baits. The world will undoubtedly be a better place.

Field Guide to the Slug has been written to help you explore the biological and ecological worlds of our slow-moving friends, the terrestrial slugs and their snail kin, and to aid in the field identification of both the benign natives and their voracious, nonnative counterparts. The emphasis throughout this book is on firsthand observation, both indoors and out. For my fellow gardeners, I've also included a section on safe, nontoxic methods of slug control.

In creating this text, I've drawn from the published works of several noted zoologists, including Branley A. Branson, Henry Pilsbry, C. David Rollo, Alan Solem, and fellow Washingtonian Dr. Eugene Kozloff. I am indebted to all of these scholars. I am also grateful to Dr. Ingrith Deyrup-Olsen, professor emeritus of zoology at the University of Washington; Klaus Richter of the King County (Washington) Resource Planning Section; and Roland Anderson of the Seattle Aquarium. Special thanks goes to Philip Dickey of the Washington Toxics Coalition for his guidance on pesticide-free slug controls.

"To err is human; to slime, sublime."

—David George Gordon

The Slug Family Tree

Land snails used to live in the ocean, but moved ashore. Since nobody told them otherwise, they expected the land to be as wet as the water. We all make mistakes.

—Will Cuppy, *How to Attract the Wombat*

Don't sell them short: Slugs and snails belong to one of the most successful groups of animals on our planet, the phylum Mollusca. The estimated 100,000 living species in this huge phylum share some important characteristics; namely, they are all invertebrates (animals without backbones), they have soft bodies, and most have hard shells made of calcium. Familiar mollusks include oysters, clams, octopuses, squid, conchs, and cowries.

Although the Mollusca are divided into seven different classes, two of these classes—the Bivalvia (oysters and clams) and the Gastropoda (slugs and snails)—constitute 99 percent of all living mollusks. However, only the Gastropoda have managed to make much of a life for themselves on dry land. With a few exceptions, the land-dwelling gastropods belong to the sub-class Pulmonata, the pulmonate land slugs and land snails. These creatures use lungs instead of gills to draw oxygen from the air.

While markedly less complex than a human lung, the lung of a pulmonate slug or snail is far from being a simple sac. In both its cellular makeup and overall function, it parallels the lungs of several higher forms of life, including at least one air-breathing vertebrate, the newt.

More than two thousand species of pulmonate slugs and snails exist worldwide. Some, like the giant snail, *Achatina achatina* of Nigeria and Guinea, are quite massive, wearing great brownish whorled shells 11 inches (28 cm) or more in diameter. Others are minuscule. The dwarf snail, *Punctum*

SLUG FAMILY TREE

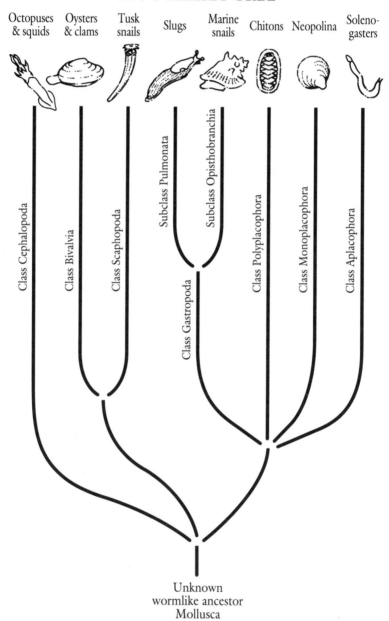

Octopuses & squids — Oysters & clams — Tusk snails — Slugs — Marine snails — Chitons — Neopolina — Soleno-gasters

Class Cephalopoda — Class Bivalvia — Class Scaphopoda — Subclass Pulmonata — Subclass Opisthobranchia — Class Gastropoda — Class Polyplacophora — Class Monoplacophora — Class Aplacophora

Unknown
wormlike ancestor
Mollusca

pygmaeum of northern Europe, for example, is comfortably housed in a flat shell less than an eighth of an inch (3 mm) in diameter.

Several pulmonate species come equipped with shells that are too small to house their sluglike bodies effectively. Evolutionary intermediates between land snails and land slugs, these oddities are called semislugs. Other pulmonates lack shells altogether or sport tiny, caplike rudimentary shells, in some instances concealed within the animal's skin. It is this group of pulmonates that scientists call the true slugs—that is, the shell-less snails.

Unlike snails, which need rich sources of calcium to construct their shells, slugs can successfully occupy a broader range of habitats, including those with volcanic, calcium-poor soils. However, slugs are more prone than snails to desiccation, and therefore are more dependent on moisture to survive. Wherever there are volcanic activity, wet weather conditions, and plenty of plant life on which to feed (for example, on the island of Borneo or throughout the Pacific Northwest), you are likely to find large numbers of slugs.

Because land slugs evolved from several different ancestral stocks, and because fossilized remains of these soft-bodied animals are nearly impossible to find, it has been difficult to compile an accurate family tree for the many thousands of living species. Presently, most are placed within two suborders of the order Stylommatophora, with these suborders further divided into ten families. Not every family has representatives in North America. The humpbacked, hook-tailed members of the slug family Urocyclidae, for example, are found only in continental Africa and Madagascar.

In the Pacific Northwest, three slug families garner the lion's share of attention: the Arionidae (which include the banana slug, *Ariolimax columbianus*, and European black slug, *Arion ater*); the Limacidae (represented by the great gray garden slug, *Limax maximus* and the milky slug, *Deroceras reticulatum*); and the Milacidae (the so-called greenhouse slugs of the genus *Milax*). Members of these families are often encountered by the avid gardener or casual slug observer in this part of the world.

The Slug in Brief

KINGDOM: *Animalia*

PHYLUM: *Mollusca*

CLASS: *Gastropoda*

SUBCLASS: *Pulmonata*

ORDER: *Stylommatophora*

SUBORDER: *Sigmurethra*

FAMILIES: *Testacellidae, Urocyclidae, Parmacellidae, Milacidae, Limacidae, Trigonochlamydidae, Boettgerillidae, Arionidae, Philomycidae*

LENGTH

One-half inch (13 mm) to ten inches (25.4 cm), depending on species.

LIFE SPAN

One to six years, depending on species.

FOOD

Whatever the forest and field have to offer: fungi, lichens, green plants, worms, centipedes, certain insects, animal feces, carrion, other slugs.

EGGS

Usually small, less than ¼ inch (6 mm) in diameter, often with a thick outer shell of calcium carbonate; laid in clutches of 3 to 50, with some species laying as many as 500 eggs per year.

PREDATORS

Small mammals, snakes, amphibians, some birds, carnivorous beetles, other slugs, and humans.

11

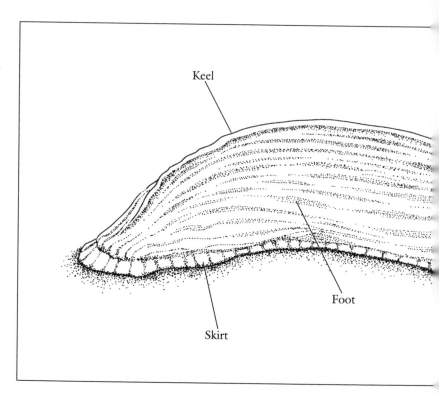

Keel

Foot

Skirt

Anatomy of a Slug

MANTLE   Also called the pallium, the mantle
is fleshy lobe that, in other gastropods,
secretes materials for making a shell.
In most slugs this anatomical feature
is vestigial; however, it can serve as
a key identifier for many species.

KEEL   A prominent ridge that runs along
the back of some slug species. Also
called the carina.

PNEUMOSTOME   A small hole or slit on the slug's right
side, leading to the slug's single lung.

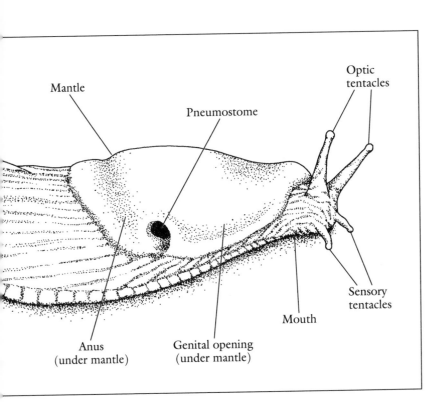

Mantle

Pneumostome

Optic tentacles

Sensory tentacles

Mouth

Anus (under mantle)

Genital opening (under mantle)

TENTACLES	Erroneously called antennae, these are two pairs of stalks—short **sensory tentacles** for feeling or smelling and longer **optic tentacles** tipped with tiny, light-sensitive eyes.
MOUTH	Located below the eyes on the underside of the head; equipped with a tonguelike, rasping radula and a jaw.
ANUS	Under a flap on the right side of the mantle; channels waste from the intestine and kidney.

GENITAL OPENING	On the right side, covered by the mantle flap. Connected to three separate internal duct systems—one for outgoing sperm, one for incoming sperm, and one for the passage of eggs to the outside.
FOOT	Broad and muscular, running the full length of the slug's dorsal surface; in some species fringed with a rippling **skirt**. Enables the slug to attain top speeds of 0.025 mile per hour.

A Gastropod Gallery: Familiar Slugs of the Northwest

Why is the Pacific Northwest graced with so many different species of slugs? The fact is, many of these are relatively new arrivals. The most commonly encountered forms have been introduced over the last two centuries, hitchhikers on plant bulbs from Holland and Germany and on produce from England, Belgium, France, and the eastern United States. Having no natural enemies here, these uninvited guests have multiplied and prospered—in many instances at the expense of our less aggressive native species' well-being.

Even excluding introduced species, however, this part of the planet boasts exceptional richness in slugs. One evolutionary hotbed for gastropods is the Olympic Peninsula—a wet, heavily forested, and largely undeveloped portion of Washington State. By conservative counts, more than 70 gastropod species currently occupy this fertile ground. Among these 70 species are 23 different species of slugs.

Following are some of the more commonly encountered slug species in the Pacific Northwest.

BANANA SLUG

The banana slug, native to the Northwest, can grow to a length of 8 inches (20 cm), with a few giants reaching 10 inches (25.4 cm), and weights of a quarter pound (0.1 kg). (The illustration represents a small, 6½-inch version of this species.) This mega-mollusk (genus *Ariolimax*) is the second-largest slug in the world, falling short by 2 inches of the ash black slug, *Limax cinereoniger* of Europe. The banana slug's color ranges from dead white to black, with many intermediate color forms—lemon yellow, light tan, and dark brown—often with black blotches or spots. In the early 1900s, each color variation was described as a new species. Today, though, only three species of banana slugs are recognized by scientists: *Ariolimax columbianus, A. dolichophallus*, and *A. californicus*. The most widely distributed of the three is *A. columbianus*, which lives almost exclusively in forested habitats of southeast Alaska, British Columbia, Washington, Oregon, and northern California. These three species are not usually encountered in urban areas.

Any slug watcher unable to identify the banana slug by its coloring, great size, or preference for woodland locales should look for a third distinguishing trait, a small indent (called the caudal pore) at the tip of the slug's tail, typically capped with a mucous plug. The mucus from this pore seems to deter rear-end attacks from shrews, shrew-moles, and predaceous beetles. It's apparently not too much of a deterrent for *Ariolimax*, however, which if particularly hungry will eat its own plug or, prior to pairing off, nibble at the plug of a prospective mate.

EUROPEAN BLACK SLUG

Arion ater, the European black slug, comes in many colors besides black. The numerous ridges and furrows behind the mantle of this slug are better identifiers than its color. Reddish brown members of the species sport a striped red-orange skirt. A bit more than half the size of the biggest banana slug (5¾ inches or 15 cm) when in motion, the European black slug will hump itself into an even smaller hillock when at rest. It will also curl into a ball and rock back and forth when under attack. It has been estimated that, at times, *Arion ater* has damaged more than 75 percent of Washington's strawberry crop.

In some parts of Washington's Mount Baker National Forest, the European black slugs outnumber the banana slugs two-to-one.

Several smaller *Arion* species (under 1½ inches or 4 cm) also exist in the Northwest: *A. circumscriptus, A. hortensis,* and *A. intermedius. A. hortensis* is quite cosmopolitan, practically a domestic animal, rarely seen outside gardens and metropolitan parks.

GREAT GRAY GARDEN SLUG

Frequently encountered in West Coast gardens,
Limax maximus comes by its common name
honestly. Sporting leopardlike spots or
tiger stripes on its mantle and the
upper surface of its foot, the
great gray garden
slug can be
distinguished
up close
by its smooth, furrowless
body and the placement of the
pneumostome, which, unlike the European
black slug's, is located near the rear edge of the mantle.
Although considerably smaller than the banana slug, this 4-inch
(10 cm) invader from Asia Minor and Europe can crawl four
times faster. In the Northwest, it is one of a handful of canni-
balistic slugs (perhaps giving the comparatively mild-mannered
native slugs a good reason to race). If you find a dying slug
on a city sidewalk at sunup, it might not be just a stray caught
by the morning sun but perhaps a victim of a great gray
garden slug attack.

MILKY SLUG

An import from northern Europe and Asia, the milky slug
(*Deroceras reticulatum*) is about 2 inches (5 cm) long, gener-
ally light brown or gray, with darker mottling and a boatlike
keel that ends abruptly at the
tail. Some specimens are
almost white. A distinct
feature of this species is its
milky slime, which it produces
in copious quantities when irritated. An equally strong identifier is the series of small, concentric folds in the mantle.

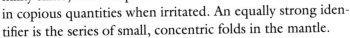

Like the European black slug, the milky slug has become a serious pest in parts of Washington and Oregon. It can slither its way into the center of a cabbage and then gorge itself on the walls of the vegetable. Milky slugs have been indicted for damage to grain fields, strawberries, and vegetable crops in the Puyallup Valley of Washington and the Willamette Valley of Oregon.

As its name implies, the **midget milky slug** (*Deroceras agreste*), while a bit shorter, has an appetite just as grand. The **marsh slug** (*D. laeve*) is the only member of this genus that is native to the Northwest. Its slime is clear.

GREENHOUSE SLUG

This drab gray slug (*Milax gagates*) is actually a true world traveler, with specimens discovered in locales as remote as Easter Island. Unintentionally carried to the Northwest from Mediterranean climes, the greenhouse slug thrives in a warm, stable environment, making it the scourge of indoor gardeners throughout the Northwest. Even if you leave the door to your greenhouse wide open, this slug will seldom venture outside. Rather, it will burrow into the first few inches of greenhouse soil and feast almost exclusively on the roots of your favorite plants. A key identifier for this species is a sharp dorsal keel that runs from the mantle to the tip of the tail. Look for a small horseshoe- or diamond-shaped groove in the center of the mantle. Like all members of their genus, greenhouse slugs sport the rudiments of a small spiral shell, completely enclosed by the skin of the mantle. Freshly hatched Milacids are fully enclosed in this shell, but they soon outgrow it in their rush to become 2¾-inch (7 cm) adults.

THREE LESS FAMILIAR GENERA

A handful of native Northwest slugs are rarely observed
by gardeners and only occasionally discovered by hikers and
campers in wilderness locales. However, their unusual behav-
iors and physical traits make them worthy of mention. Slugs
of the genus *Prophysaon* have gained a reputation for what
scientists call autotomy—that is, when attacked by a predator,
they can jettison part of their tail. A yellow-green mucus is
secreted on the front section of the body at the site of the
attack. Assumed to be a deterrent, this sticky substance may
divert further attacks from the body and toward the detached
tail. Ideally, the 2¼-inch-long (6 cm) slug will then make its
escape. Under laboratory conditions, a new tail is regenerated
in approximately five weeks. The autotomized section is
packed with glycogen cells, stored nutrients that can be used
by the slug if food is unavailable.

Dark gray with lateral bands of color, *Prophysaon vanattae*
is the most widespread and abundant member of this genus
on the mainland of Washington and British Columbia. The
reticulated gray *P. andersoni*, according to naturalist Robert
Michael Pyle, "shows a liking for wild mushrooms, especially
chanterelles." The slightly smaller *P. foliolatum* is typically
yellowish, with a light stripe down its back and several dark
brown streaks and spots. However, specimens collected from
a single leaf of skunk cabbage on the Olympic coast of Washington showed a range of body colors—from very pale yellow
without markings to dark rust or brown. Therefore, it is better
to use the tail as an identifier of this and other related species.
Shaped more or less like a rounded oblong, it usually bears a
small crease marking the site where self-amputation takes place.

Considerably smaller than most Northwest native slugs (½ to
¾ inch, 13 to 20 mm), members of the genus *Hemphillia* can
be distinguished by their vestigial shells, the edges of which
are partly blurred by the skin of the mantle. These mottled

olive-and-brown natives avoid predators by resorting to invertebrate acrobatics. A resting slug will wrap its long, slender tail forward around its body. If disturbed, it will swing the tail back, twisting and writhing with such vigor that the slug often jumps an inch. The adaptive range of one species, *H. malonei*, is impressive: In Oregon, specimens have been collected deep in the Columbia Gorge and on Mount Hood at elevations up to 4,250 feet (1,295 m). A relative, *H. glandulosa*, is found solely in coastal forests.

The nonnative ***Testacella haliotidea*** is a carnivore, with a harpoonlike barbed radula for impaling earthworms and other soft-bodied prey. The catch is swallowed whole, an act that takes several hours to complete. Much of this slug's life is spent underground. Its small size—less than 2½ inches (6 cm)—and subdued gray-brown or pale yellow skin make it easy to overlook. One characteristic stands out, however: a small, caplike shell resembling that of an abalone. It is from this feature that this species of *Testacella* gets its name, *haliotidea*—a reference to the abalone genus, *Haliotis*.

A Few Words About Snails

The formal boundary between "slugdom" and "snaildom" is somewhat arbitrary. However, few of us would have any trouble pegging the snail in a lineup of slugs. The obvious difference, of course, is the shell.

A hard shell made of calcium is a wonderful device for ensuring a long, successful life on land. It protects the wearer from most predators and, especially important for an otherwise naked land dweller, guards against drying up. Many land snails can withdraw into their shells for days or even months, sealing off the opening with a thin layer of calcium and hardened mucus. The snail then goes into a long-term state of suspended animation. Thus protected, it can wait out a cold snap or

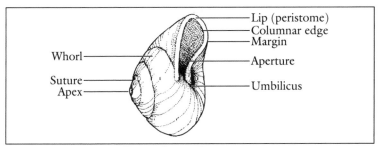

Labels: Whorl, Suture, Apex, Lip (peristome), Columnar edge, Margin, Aperture, Umbilicus

LAND SNAIL SHELL

drought, returning to an active life with the first warm rains. The record for such a wait is shared by a pair of Mexican desert snail species, a few specimens of which survived for six years in a box, stuck in a desk drawer belonging to a San Francisco scientist.

Without its shell, one Northwest snail species looks pretty much like the next. Therefore, identification is usually based on the attributes of each snail's shell. Describing these characteristics means learning the language of conchology, the study of mollusk shells. A few basic terms are presented here.

All Northwest land snail shells are **turbinate**—that is, they grow at an angle along a spiral screw. Each circular turn of this screw is known as a **whorl**, and the tip of the spire is called its **apex**. The juncture of each whorl against the other forms a **suture**. The circular hollow created by the spiraling whorls is the **umbilicus**. The **aperture** is the opening into which a live snail can retreat. The edge of the body whorl that borders the aperture is known as the **lip** or, more technically, the **peristome**. The **columnar edge** is the inner edge of this lip, and the outer edge is the **margin**.

With the exception of an occasional mutant, all Northwest turbinate shells are **dextral**—that is, the bulk of the shell is worn rather jauntily on the soft body's right side. If you should happen to find a left-sided shell, hang on to it. It could be valuable, if not to science then at least to an amateur collector.

NONNATIVE SNAIL SPECIES

As with Northwest slugs, the introduced snail species garner most of our attention. The **brown garden snail** (*Helix aspersa*) was the first foreign mollusk to be introduced into western North America, allegedly during the 1850s by a French epicure who lived in San Francisco (and who actually longed for the taste of a second gourmet gastropod, *H. pomatia*, the **European apple snail**). Large numbers of brown garden snail shells have been found in kitchen waste among Roman ruins in Great Britain, and both Pliny the Elder and Varro mention the special vessels in which these edible snails were kept. Napoleon's soldiers carried canned edible snails as emergency rations during their great campaigns, "the extract of 1,000 snails per man" being sufficient fare for one week. Brown garden snails continue to make frequent appearances, usually in garlic butter, throughout England, Italy, and France. Live specimens are routinely found by gardeners throughout the Northwest.

The light brown shell of this species is conical with a blunt spire, irregularly marked with growth lines and sculpted with folds, barely more than 1⅛ inches (2.9 cm) in diameter. Its white-lipped margin has an outwardly bent edge; the umbilicus is completely covered by the columnar edge. In winter months, the brown garden snail seals the opening of its shell. As a result, these snails are said to taste best in spring, when the calcium salt content of the flesh is lowest. In snails collected and cooked during winter months, these salts are precipitated, giving the flesh an undesirable flavor. "Strange to say, epicures who like snails for food seem to prefer them from imported cans from Europe rather than picking them from western gardens," offers G. Dallas Hanna, whose 1966 monograph *Introduced Mollusks of Western North America* remains invaluable for snail sorters to this day.

The **brown-lipped** or **grove snail** (*Cepaea nemoralis*) came to the Northwest from western Europe, but not before establishing itself in gardens throughout the eastern United States. "In 1857, I imported some hundred living specimens from near Sheffield, England, and freed them in my garden in Burlington, New Jersey," wrote one avid gardener in 1865. "They have thriven well and increased with great rapidity, so that now the whole town is full of them." There have been many accidental introductions of this beautifully colored land snail since then. Shells of this species come in shades of red, yellow, and olive, with one to five bands of cinnamon to chocolate brown hues. The shell's brown lip usually distinguishes its wearer from *C. hortensis*, an equally common introduced species in the Northwest.

The **garlic snail** (*Oxychilus alliarius*) is a ¼-inch (6 mm) member of a large European family of thin-shelled mollusks called glass snails. Like a skunk, it has the potential for producing a disagreeable odor when provoked. The garlic snail is completely dependent on humankind, enjoying the comfort of our greenhouses, cold frames, and cloches. Its glossy amber or horn-colored shell is streaked with dull gray and includes four to six rather flat whorls. Look for a small but obvious umbilicus. The **cellar snail** (*O. cellarius*) is nearly identical in appearance but lacks the odor. Both species are primarily flesh eaters.

NATIVE SNAIL SPECIES

Native snail species are too seldom encountered to warrant common names, and, as they spend most of their time in forests, they have made relatively few enemies among gardeners. Nonetheless, they are occasionally found in garden tracts, particularly those on the urban fringe. Know them as natives and treat them with some respect.

Monadenia fidelis can be recognized by its 1¼-inch (3.2 cm) nut-brown shell, streaked with light bands, dark bands, or both.

Haplotrema sportella has a greenish yellow shell roughly a half-inch (1.3 cm) in diameter, with a flattened spire and a pronounced concavity on one edge of its aperture lip. It shares its range (from northern California to Alaska) with a second species, *H. vancouverensis*, which shows little indentation of the aperture lip.

In the living snail, the brown, ¾-inch-diameter (2 cm) shell of *Vespericola columbiana* is covered with fine hairs. The hairs fall off after the animal dies; in these hairless specimens, look for the aperture's thickened lip.

Allogona townsendiana is a relative of *Vespericola*, and its 1-inch (2.5 cm) diameter shell shares the same thickening of the lip. The gnarly whorls of its polished pecan brown shell are often eroded, revealing a whitish, limy undercoat.

The Seven Wonders of Slugdom

SOLE

Latin for "stomach-foot," the term *gastropod* refers to the basic body plan of all slugs and snails. The stomach and, for that matter, most of a slug's guts are contained in a broad, muscular foot. The bottom of this foot (the part that touches the ground) is called the sole. In some species, the sole's outer edge is fringed with a skirt of flesh, often brightly colored or striped.

So how does a slug get around with just one foot? To answer that question, try this experiment: Place a slug on a piece of plate glass, let it settle for a few minutes, then watch it from beneath the glass. As the slug creeps across the smooth surface, you'll see a rippling pattern of alternating dark- and light-colored bands running the length of the sole, flowing in waves from the tail to the head. Should the slug come to a halt, the waves will stop.

Those light and dark bands represent oblique muscle fibers, relaxing and contracting in what are technically known as pedal

CROSS-SECTION OF A SLUG'S FOOT

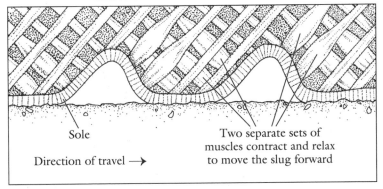

Sole

Direction of travel →

Two separate sets of muscles contract and relax to move the slug forward

waves. There are actually two sets of these muscle fibers, each performing separate chores. To move forward, one set—those fibers directed inward and rearward—contracts between waves, pulling the slug from the front and pushing off toward the back. Simultaneously, the second set—the fibers directed inward and forward—pulls the outer surface of the sole forward, generating each pedal wave. In several of the larger Northwest slug species, this second set of muscle fibers can generate as many as 18 waves at a time—quite an interesting show when viewed from below.

SLIME

As you watch a slug move across the glass, you can't miss the trail of slime left in its wake. The slime comes from the pedal gland, a large funnel-shaped opening at the front of the foot (right beneath the head), and from the sole. Slug slime (more politely described as mucus) plays a crucial role in the animal's efforts at getting around, simultaneously increasing traction and greasing the skids, as it were. In most slug species, two kinds of mucus are produced by the pedal gland. The first is free-flowing, spread laterally over the surface of the sole; the second is extra viscous and is passed backward along the full length of the sole. Both substances are flattened by the slug as it travels, producing those all-too-familiar silvery trails on our patios and garden paths.

In his studies of locomotion in the banana slug, one British Columbian researcher discovered that resting slugs could remain attached to a rock wall or other vertical surface for many hours, despite what one would assume to be the natural tendency of any slime-coated creature to slowly slide to the ground. He found that the mucus under these resting slugs contained a dense network of fine, long fibers that limited the slime's lubricity by slowing its flow. How these fibers are formed has yet to be determined.

It is not just the sole of a slug that can leave a slime trail. Virtually the entire body surface produces mucus—the mantle, the area surrounding the pneumostome, a groove around the edge of the foot, the head, and, in some species, the caudal gland at the base of the tail. Different kinds of mucus are used for self-defense, moisture control, and mating. When threatened, most slugs secrete an especially thick coating, making them harder to grasp. This thick mucus can gum up the works, actually sealing the mouths of snakes or shrews or causing larger predators such as ducks or dogs to gag.

Slug mucus absorbs water, helping to prevent dehydration—a serious threat to any terrestrial creature of aquatic ancestry. This is one reason that slug slime is nearly impossible to wash off. Rubbing your hands under running water only makes things worse; the slime should be wiped off with a dry towel before you wash. Or try rubbing your dry hands together, in much the same way you'd remove rubber cement. The slime can be rolled into a ball and discarded.

With its protective covering of mucus, a slug can slide along the edge of a razor blade or crawl across crushed glass. Some, like the banana slug, can even suspend themselves from a slender but strong slime cord, slowly lowering themselves headfirst from the branches of trees or shrubs to reach the ground. The great gray garden slug employs a similar mucous thread to mate in midair.

Slugs also seem to use mucus for navigation, employing their keen sense of smell to follow the chemical constituents of slime trails. In this way they can seek mates, stalk other slugs, or simply find their way home. According to researcher C. David Rollo, "A slug can find its own shelter from more than 3 feet away by following the odor of its droppings within the crevice and, perhaps, by the scent of a special slime it exudes while resting." One individually marked banana slug was observed leaving a hole in spring and returning to the same hole in autumn. In *The Descent of Man and Selection in Relation to Sex*, Charles Darwin reported on the pulmonate predisposition for slime-tracking: "An accurate observer, Mr. Lonsdale, informs me that he placed a pair of land snails (*Helix pomatia*), one of which was weakly, into a small and ill-provided garden. After a short time, the strong and healthy individual disappeared and was traced by its track of slime over a wall into an adjoining well-stocked garden. Mr. Lonsdale concluded that it had deserted its sickly mate; but after an absence of twenty-four hours it returned and apparently communicated the result of its successful exploration, for both then started along the same track and disappeared over the wall."

STOMACH

It would seem that slugs live to eat. Most of their active hours are spent seeking and devouring fungi, lichens, algae, the soft parts of plants both below and above the ground, other slugs, a few insects, animal feces, and carrion. All other activities seem to be secondary. Many slugs consume several times their own body weight each day.

Naturally, a slug's insides reflect this consuming passion. Filling a large part of the body cavity is an expandable sac called a crop, within which enzymes from paired salivary glands help break down the slug's fiber-rich diet. The partially processed food enters a smaller, pouchlike stomach, where hepatic enzymes from another set of glands turn the food into mush. The mush passes from the great digestive gland (or liver) and from there into a long, looped intestine, which opens to the outside world via the anus on the slug's right side. By the time waste leaves the slug, as much as 90 percent of its nutritive value has been assimilated. Slug droppings are wrapped in (what else?) mucus and make great food for nearby plants, assuming that any plants are left once the slug finishes its meal.

How a slug's food gets into the crop is another interesting story. To feed, the slug first extends its mouth, then uses its jaw—a solid structure that drops like a guillotine—to latch onto a lichen, leaf, or whatever. Then with its radula (a ribbon-like body part unique to mollusks, bearing as many as 27,000 sharp, backward-pointing teeth), it rasps at the plant material. Like sharks, slugs routinely lose and replace their teeth, with new ones coming from the rear of the radula. (The radula also is employed in slug-to-slug combat; if you look closely, you may see tiny dueling scars on the more aggressive slug species, usually acquired during territorial disputes.) The pulp is passed back into the esophagus. It gets mixed with saliva and mucus, then flows into the crop.

SPEED (OR LACK THEREOF)

They don't call them slugs for nothing. The swiftest of pulmonates, shelled or unshelled, will never win a race against a box turtle, even an elderly, three-legged one. Take, for example, that big-footed loper, the banana slug, which has been clocked at 6½ inches (16.5 cm) per minute, or 32½ feet (10 m) per hour. At this rate, the creature would finish the 100-yard dash in a little under 9 hours and 15 minutes, assuming it didn't stop for a snack along the way. As mentioned earlier, however, the great gray garden slug can easily overtake a banana slug on the run. With food as a motivator, even the smallest of slugs can cover great distances. The milky slug, for example, will travel up to 40 feet (12.2 m) in a single night to get its fill. Although slow, slugs and snails are remarkably strong. In laboratory tests, one species was able to drag 50 times its own weight horizontally and 9 times its weight vertically.

SENSES

They may be sluggish, but no one can say they are out of touch with their environment. A slug's body is dotted with sensory cells, enabling this quiet browser to taste and smell, and react to light and darkness from all angles. These cells are most densely clustered around the mouth and tentacles and at several locations along the length of the foot.

The slug's insides are also equipped with sense receptors. These minute internal monitors send signals to the slug's command module (not really a brain, as we humans tend to use this word, but a ring of nine large nerve ganglia) to initiate or terminate feeding behavior.

The ganglia also process information from the slug's two pairs of tentacles—hollow muscular tubes that can move telescopically, in or out, up or down, as the need arises. These tentacles can operate independently, letting the slug gather information from several directions at the same time. The shorter pair are called sensory tentacles. Cast toward the ground, they help the slug sample its world at close range by smell and taste. The longer optic tentacles extend upward and are tipped with oval-shaped eyes, each fitted with a crude retina and lens. Although unable to perceive detailed images, these eyes can distinguish light from dark at a distance. One study of the milky slug revealed a second retina on each optic tentacle, possibly an infrared receptor for detecting and avoiding sources of heat.

SEX

In the ocean, many mollusks release sperm and eggs into the water, then sit back and let them drift around until they find each other. But on land, such a laissez-faire approach to sex is not likely to pay off. Hence, land slugs and snails have developed complicated mating routines and enlarged reproductive organs to make sure that their eggs and sperm wind up where they are supposed to.

Although slugs are hermaphroditic, each animal equipped with both male and female reproductive organs, they mate with themselves only if no other slugs are around. Given a choice, they seek partners with which to trade genetic material, a move that, by favoring the passage of chromosomes from both parents to the offspring, nurtures a healthier pool of slug genes. The actual exchange of sperm is preceded by an elaborate courtship ritual, which supposedly reduces the chances of two individuals of separate species mating and giving rise to hybrids.

During courtship, two slugs will circle each other, often for hours, with both partners engaged in ritualized bouts of lunging, nipping, and sideswiping with their tails. The two slugs may also display their disproportionately large sex organs. The great gray garden slug's penis is nearly half its total body length. In fact, penis size is reflected in the scientific name of one banana slug species: *dolichophallus*— Latin for "long penis."

MATING SLUGS
(*LIMAX MAXIMUS*)

"The sight of a courting pair of slugs majestically circling one another and ceremoniously rasping each other's flanks while they solemnly wave their enormous penises overhead puts the most improbably athletic couples of Pompeii and Khajuraho into a more appropriate and severely diminished perspective," note researchers C. David Rollo and William G. Wellington. "Athletic" is an even more appropriate adjective for great gray garden slugs, which are able to copulate in midair, suspended by stretchy strands of mucus up to 17¾ inches (45 cm) long.

As courtship progresses, a banana slug pair intertwines, wrapping themselves in an "S" position and stimulating each other for several more hours. Their genital areas (immediately in front of the pneumostome) swell as the pair move even closer together. Penetration takes place, then each slug alternately releases and receives sperm.

But in the case of the banana slug, that's hardly the end of this amazing routine. Now the slugs must disengage—a challenge for two animals so amply endowed and thoroughly covered in sticky mucus. After long bouts of writhing and pulling, the pair may resort to what scientists call apophallation. Translated, this means that one slug gnaws off the penis of the other.

Is there an advantage to such odd behavior? Yes, according to Adrian Forsyth, author of *A Natural History of Sex*. The apophallated slug, says Forsyth, "cannot regrow his penis and is now obligated to be a female and forced to offer eggs. It may be that the castrator can raise his reproductive success by increasing locally the density of females." Slug scientist Albert Mead has suggested that apophallation may be nature's way of maintaining the species. After all, he writes, in other animal species, gigantism has been a precursor to extinction. Only by submitting to the shears can banana slugs maintain their inordinate organs.

Admittedly, slug mating may seem bizarre by our standards. The slug's egg-laying, however, is no more extraordinary than that of a chicken. Transparent, golden, or pearly white round or oval-shaped eggs are deposited in clutches of anywhere from 3 to 50, usually beneath a piece of wood or debris or in a small crevice or hole in the ground. Banana slugs seldom lay more than 40 eggs at a time, but the European garden slug and several other species can lay larger numbers with greater frequency, so that individual slugs may deposit as many as 500 fertile eggs in a year.

Depending on weather and soil conditions (slugs will not lay their eggs when water saturation in the soil is below 10 percent), slug eggs hatch in three to eight weeks. Eggs that are laid in late autumn usually overwinter and hatch the next spring. The hatchlings look like miniature adults but lack the defense mechanisms of their parents, so they are extremely vulnerable to predators. They grow quickly, however, and move beyond this dangerous stage after a few months. By the end of a season, they are often indistinguishable from their parents.

SPECIATION

Naturalist Branley A. Branson has ascribed the proliferation of Northwest slug species to changes in climatic conditions in the ancient past. During the warmer, moister periods of the Mesozoic era, roughly 200 million years ago, slugs from Asia crept or were carried into a new, largely unexploited world. Inch by inch, one century after the next, these soft-bodied settlers pushed southward into what is now Mexico. At the same time, slugs from South and Central America expanded their range northward. This resulted in a mixing of northern and southern species along the western edge of the continent. "That Asian elements were actually able to penetrate into North America is attested by the fact that the nearest relative of the western American slug genus *Prophysaon* is found in east and central Asia," Branson writes.

Slugs continued to mingle until the late Pliocene epoch (2 or 3 million years ago), when the climate again changed and southern and northern species returned to their respective corners. Members of one slug genus, *Binneya*, which had originally migrated northward as far as today's Washington, Idaho, and southern Canada, were wiped out in the cold north. The descendants of these slugs are now found in only one place, on Santa Barbara Island, off the Southern California coast.

Glaciers (whose movement was a phenomenon with which even slugs could keep pace) also contributed to the demise of many slugs, covering their habitats in layers of ice and leaving remnant populations stranded in the south or on mountain slopes. It was during this time that populations of the cold-adapted genus *Hemphillia* were isolated in parts of Montana, southern Canada, Oregon, and Washington—a condition, according to Branson, that ultimately produced the five species of *Hemphillia* we recognize today.

Finding Slugs in Your Garden

There are several good reasons for watching slugs. Curiosity is as good a motive as any; the better your understanding of the food web (of which both you and the slugs are a part), the greater your appreciation of nature's grand design. "When we try to pick out anything by itself, we find it hitched to everything in the universe," wrote the great American naturalist John Muir.

"Know thine enemies," a more familiar quotation, suggests another good reason for slug watching. The deeper your familiarity with the slugs' patterns for raiding your garden, the more capable you will be of limiting damage to your plants. By periodically conducting informal surveys of abundance, you should get an idea of the best control strategies. Increased numbers, especially of young slugs or snails, will be a warning that sterner controls are needed.

With a few exceptions (the banana slug, for instance, feeds by day in spring and fall), slugs are most active at night. To observe them in action, then, go into your garden after dark

CAN YOU FIND THE SLUG IN THIS GARDEN?

or shortly before sunup, armed with a flashlight or, better yet, a headlamp, which will leave both hands free for field work.

Start at the bases of your most appetizing plants and look for large, irregularly shaped holes in the leaves—a good indication that slugs or snails have dined on your foliage. If you can't catch any slugs in the act of feeding, simply follow their slime trails to nearby hiding places. Often these trails lead to ivy or other plants that slugs don't eat but that make great daytime shelters. Check other daytime hiding places, too: under luxuriant shrubs, amid stacked firewood, in tall grass, and around mulch piles, heaps of autumn leaves, or stockpiled building materials. You may get lucky and find a few slugs sleeping in. Be thorough in your investigations: It has been suggested that for each slug caught by a gardener, another 20 go undetected. Scientific studies of slug abundance on cultivated lands have produced peak estimates of 72,000 hungry mouths per acre.

You are most likely to find garden slugs during months with moderate but consistent rainfall and nighttime temperatures above 50 degrees Fahrenheit (10°C). In the Northwest, the best months to search for slugs are March, April, May, June, and October. However, even in the coldest or driest weather, it should be possible to find some evidence of nighttime feeding.

Controlling Slugs

Get up, sweet Slug-a-bed, and see
The Dew bespangling Herbe and Tree

—ROBERT HERRICK (1591–1674)
"CORINNA'S GOING A-MAYING"

Clearly, you won't be able to eliminate all of the slugs in your garden—as proved by one English zoologist who systematically removed 400 slugs from a quarter-acre garden each night for several years without any observable effect on the population. And as slugs are basically small cogs in nature's big machine, there are many good reasons why you shouldn't even try to eliminate them. Native slugs were here long before we were, so, ethically speaking, they have just as much right to pursue their private paths as we do. Unfortunately, the paths of most nonnative slugs often lead to your best lettuce or basil plants. Even more unfortunate is the tendency of many gardeners to place blame on all slugs, including the more benign woodland slug species, for the work done by the urban despoilers.

The challenge for most gardeners is to maintain a balance, something that introduced slug and snail species in particular seem to know nothing about. Nonnatives have few natural enemies, and because most of us maintain our gardens to yield bumper crops, there will never be a shortage of food for these slithering hordes. Still, if you feel the urge to maintain order, try the most humane and least environmentally damaging control measures first.

BEGIN BY ALTERING
THE ENVIRONMENT

First of all, keep slug populations down by making your property less desirable for them. This can involve choosing plants such as rhododendrons and other hard-leaved evergreens that slugs will ignore and avoiding those that slugs actively seek (a list of both kinds of plants can be found on page 47). Rid your garden of good slug hiding places, and avoid overwatering. Frequent cultivation of bare soil can destroy slug eggs before they hatch.

Some Northwest gardeners control slugs by planting horseradish, mustards, marigolds, or other greenery with high slug appeal. By regularly checking this sacrificial vegetation, you can eliminate any creatures it attracts. It is important to be ever vigilant, though, lest the slugs consider these plants appetizers and then start combing your garden for the main course.

You can also invite slug-eating predators into your yard. However, the damage to plants from unsupervised chickens, geese, and ducks can sometimes exceed that of slugs, and the presence of snakes and other slug predators may be as unsettling as that of the creatures you seek to control.

MOUNT A SLUG SAFARI

Hand-picking slugs from your plants can be an effective control, especially at night, when the slugs are most active. If you're squeamish about slime (and most people are), use a long-handled dandelion digger or a pair of long tweezers. Plop any captives into a jar filled with soapy water, which will prevent them from slipping over the top. As an extra security measure, use a jar with a screw top, as slugs have been known to push with sufficient force to pop the lid off of a yogurt container.

For severe slug infestations, recruit your neighborhood kids and offer a bounty for each slug they bring in. Remember to set a reasonable price, never more than a nickel. One Seattle gardener boasted of capturing as many as 800 slugs in one night; at 10 cents a head, he would be out 80 dollars!

TRY A FEW TRAPS

Either store-bought or built at home, slug traps offer a more passive approach to pest control. One time-honored device is the beer trap. Little more than a shallow pan or saucer with its rim flush to the ground, it employs the scent of the brew's chief constituents, malt and yeast, to lure slugs to a watery grave. Some of the best beer traps are made from plastic butter tubs or cottage cheese containers, the depth of which makes it harder for satiated slugs to escape. Cut a few 1-inch-square doors into the sides of either vessel and use the lid to deflect rain, thus preventing dilution.

While no single beer brand has been proved most effective at offing slugs, a researcher from Colorado State University has concluded that Kingsbury Malt Beverage (from Heileman

BEER TRAP

Plastic tub with lid

Door

Beer

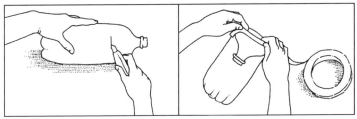

MAKING A SLUG HOTEL

Breweries) is superior for attracting snails. Adding a dash of baker's yeast has been proved to make a beer trap more effective. Avoid the impulse to empty the trap each day, as most slugs are attracted by the dead bodies of their own kind. However, because the beer in these traps will eventually sour and lose its potency, it's important to keep a fresh supply on hand. (Perhaps this is why so many gardeners are fond of beer traps!) In lieu of beer, an equally potent attractant can be concocted from two tablespoons of flour, ½ teaspoon of brewer's yeast, and one teaspoon of sugar mixed in two cups of warm water.

A very simple but rather gruesome slug trap consists of two boards, one on top of the other, separated by a few small stones. In the morning, remove the stones and stomp on the upper board, crushing any slugs or snails that have sought sanctuary there from the light of day. Other hungry slugs will be attracted by the mashed bodies, so you can repeat the procedure as often as you like.

Other effective lures for shade-loving slugs include grapefruit rinds, two-gallon flowerpots, or plastic lawn or leaf bags—preferably green—strategically placed on the soil. These lures should be checked first thing in the morning, before rising temperatures and reduced humidity force the inhabitants to seek other shelters.

A more refined trap, euphemistically called a slug hotel, can be built from an empty plastic soda pop bottle. Cut the bottle at its shoulder, just before it starts to taper toward the neck. Stick the piece you have just cut off into the bottle, neck-first. Tape the two pieces together with duct or electrical tape. Fill the trap half full with beer or apple cider and bury it sideways in your garden, so that the entrance is level with the ground. When your hotel is fully occupied, untape the top and empty its contents into your garbage can or compost bin. Refill it with beer or cider and post a "vacancy" sign.

SKIP THE SALT

Putting a dash of salt on a slug and then watching it melt— nearly every Northwesterner has tried this experiment at least once. Shame on us, though. The salt creates an ionic imbalance, which impels the animal to crawl out of its own slime and rapidly dehydrate. Because a slug's body surface contains numerous nerve endings, salting causes undue pain for the slug. In addition, too many applications will eventually make the soil toxic to all but a few salt-tolerant plants.

CORRAL SLUGS WITH COPPER

Using barriers to keep slugs from parts of your property may prove more effective than mounting a campaign of mass extermination. However, choosing the proper barrier deserves thought. Many gardeners say that rows of garlic or onion plants can act as deterrents. Others claim that paths of diatomaceous earth, wood ash, or shredded bark can impede the movement of slugs. Alas, these deterrents seem to work best during dry spells, when slugs are least likely to cross such lines anyway. Anyone who thinks the sharp edges of crushed gravel will serve as a barricade hasn't read page 27 of this book. At best, gravel dries out more quickly than topsoil, making it a less appealing medium for moisture-loving slugs.

Delphinium growers in England have reported success with aluminum sulfate crystals, sprinkled on the ground between

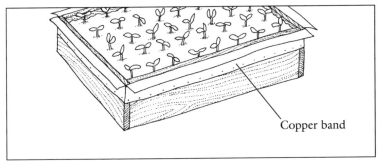

Copper band

SLUG BARRIER

plants. The crystals act as an irritant or promote dehydration in slugs. In the United States, this chemical is frequently used to induce blue flowers on hydrangeas; however, no information on its effectiveness against slugs is available.

Perhaps the best barriers are made of solid copper in bands at least 3 inches (7.5 cm) wide. A slug that comes into contact with one of these bands receives a slight electric shock. To increase effectiveness, bend the upper edge of each band over and down, forming a flange. Because copper is expensive, it becomes cost-effective to group slug-prone plants. Don't fret should your copper bands turn green with age; their effectiveness as electrified slug fences will not be affected by such oxidation.

USE YOUR IMAGINATION

Nearly every devout gardener has invented a way to keep slugs in their place. One senior horticulturist with plenty of time on his hands actually builds small bridges of bran across partially buried coffee cans filled with soapy water. Each bridge is constructed to crumble under a slug's modest weight.

Another folk invention involves putting slugs in a blender and then coating plant leaves with the resultant puree to repel other slugs. "It made sense to me," wrote Philip Dickey in *Alternatives*, the quarterly newsletter of the Washington Toxics

Coalition. "Even a slug wouldn't want to eat lettuce that had that glop all over it." Unfortunately, such a technique works only with daily applications and only on slugs of the same species as those in the glop. Concludes Dickey, "you would definitely need a second blender." Health risks from slug or snail parasites make this measure more trouble than it is worth.

RESORT TO CHEMICAL WARFARE

Many commercial slug and snail baits are available today as pellets, meal, or emulsions. Most combine an attractant (usually apple meal or some other sweet-smelling base) with an active ingredient (most commonly the chemical compound metaldehyde) to poison whatever swallows the bait. Metaldehyde works by dehydrating its victims, so, theoretically speaking, in wet weather slugs can rehydrate themselves, sloughing off a supposedly lethal dose.

Several slug bait manufacturers rely on carbamate compounds, originally developed as insecticides, to exterminate slugs. Others include a second poison, methiocarb (commercially sold as Mesurol).

Ingested metaldehyde can lead to nervous system damage or death in humans and other animals. The threshold for tolerance is related to size, making birds and small mammals especially vulnerable. Carbamates are even more toxic than metaldehyde to animals, including earthworms and other soil fauna. Because of its high toxicity to humans, methiocarb should not be used around food crops. If you decide to use baits containing any of these chemicals, use them judiciously. Usually the manufacturer's caveats will tell you more than you care to know. Here is a sample:

> Harmful if swallowed or absorbed through the skin. This pesticide may be fatal to children and dogs or other pets if eaten. Protect dogs from treated areas, since they may

be attracted to this product when applied. This product is toxic to birds and other wildlife. Birds feeding on treated areas may be killed. Do not apply directly to water or contaminate water by cleaning of equipment or disposal of wastes.

Chemicals potentially pose one other problem—how to safely dispose of slug corpses. While bodies collected from other means can be composted or flushed down the toilet, chemical-laden slugs should be buried away from your garden and any natural sources of water. This will allow most poisons to break down into harmless constituents while preventing other land animals from feeding on tainted flesh.

Observing Slugs in the Wild

John Muir wrote that "in every walk with nature, one receives far more than he seeks." Indeed, by watching slugs in a garden, you're likely to learn only the habits of pesky introduced species, which are more comfortable in backyard beds. Searching for slugs in a forest or field may require more time and effort, but it can reward you with glimpses of Northwest native slugs in their rightful places. Only by observing these well-adapted animals in a natural setting can we understand the slugs' many ecological functions. As "Nature's Slimy Helpers," wild slugs hasten decomposition of organic matter, fertilize the soil, and assist in the dispersal of seeds and spores. The whole forest benefits from their presence.

As most native slugs are solitary by nature, there is a greater likelihood of encountering single specimens than whole herds. Nonetheless, once you've discovered a woodland slug's favorite spot, you can revisit it over several seasons, as most slugs are territorial—that is, they tend to stay within easy crawling distance of a cozy den.

Many slugs show a strong attachment to particular shelters during hot or dry weather, but tend to relocate during cool, moist weather. Comfortably wedged in a rock crevice or beneath a stone or a log, the banana slug can wait out a dry spell, remaining in a torpid state for more than three months. At higher altitudes, slugs of the genus *Prophysaon* may remain cooped up in a hollow log for as long as six or seven months. If you find either of these stay-at-homes in their dormant states, let them be. Forcing them out of their torpor could cost them their lives.

Adult banana slugs have a rather long reproductive period, from late summer through early spring, a period that coincides with the Northwest's wet months. This means that pint-size baby bananas may be observed during all but the relatively dry months of July, August, and September.

Watching Slugs at Home

They don't claw like cats or screech like parrots and, unlike dogs, they won't demand to be taken for walks. Have you considered keeping a slug for a pet?

Begin with a fish tank, 10 gallons (38 l) or larger. Cover the base of the tank with an inch (2.5 cm) of pea gravel, then add an inch or two of potting soil. Now decorate with moss, leaf litter, and twigs. Add a couple of pieces of tree bark, a few rocks, or some pot shards to make hiding places; these hide-outs will encourage your slugs to stay put, instead of roaming and sliming the slug-arium's glass. Slime trails will eventually obscure your view, so it's best to remove them, preferably with a dry or slightly moistened paper towel or a razor blade (using a wet sponge or squeegee will only make matters worse).

Make sure you buy or build a snug-fitting screen top for the tank, as without it your pets should have no difficulty climbing straight up and out. The screen top will allow air to circulate, keeping the tank fresh. Because slugs favor damp conditions, at least half of the screening should be covered with cardboard or foil, to keep some moisture in. From time to time, you may want to spray your slug's home with a plant mister.

If for no other reasons than its spectacular size and docile temperament, a banana slug is a good pet for a child. They are extremely heat-sensitive, though, making them less suited to captive lifestyles than the Northwest's many introduced slug species. If you want to bring one or two banana slugs into your home, keep their tank on an unheated porch or in a garage. They should be brought indoors during severe cold spells and returned only when the temperatures are well above freezing.

More tolerant of heat, the great gray garden slug makes a better pet. To avoid territorial battles in their new home, choose young specimens that are roughly the same size, provide them with separate hiding places, and make sure that food is always available. A drawback to this slug is, alas, its nocturnal nature: The most entertaining moments are likely to occur at night, when no one's around to notice.

Pet slugs should be offered a broad spectrum of foods—spinach, lettuce, and other leafy greens—augmented with fresh browse, harvested from the outdoors. One pet owner maintains that her slugs have a fondness for yams but tend to reject scraps of sweet potato or regular potato. Another reports his slug's preference for wild-harvested mushrooms and the leaves of the devil's club plant, *Oplopanax horridum*. Other gastropod staples include dry kibbled dog food, poultry mash, and pelleted salmon chow. Don't assume that all slug fare must be fresh; in most cases, overripe and wilted fruits and vegetables (which often can be obtained free of charge from produce stands) will be eaten with gusto.

Pet slugs have few medical disorders, so it is altogether possible for your pet to live as long as several years, depending on the species. Like everyone else, slugs are susceptible to bacterial infections, but these are not transmittable to humans or other endothermic (warm-blooded) occupants of your home. Some slug species are intermediate hosts to such parasites as tapeworms and flukes, and for this reason alone, it is never a good idea to put a slug in your mouth!

Plants Slugs Avoid Eating

Agapanthus
Alocasia
Anemone japonica
   or nemorosa
Arum italicum
Aspidistra
Astilbe
Baby's tears
Bamboo
Bedding begonias
Begonia 'Cleopatra'
Bleeding heart
Bromeliads
Campanula poscharskyana
Coral bells
Cyclamen
Dichondra
Duchenesea
Endymion hispanicus
Epimedium (taller species)
Evergreen candy tuft
Ferns
Foxglove
Galium odoratum
Gaultheria
Hedychium
Impatiens
Ivy
Juniper
Kenilworth ivy
Linnaea
London pride
Nandina
Oxalis oregona
Sansevieria
Sedum (except S. maximus)
Sempervivum
Solomon's seal
Taxus
Thalictrum
Thymus serpyllum
Viola hederacea or rupestris
Wandering Jew

Plants Slugs Love to Eat

Asarum
Athyrium goeringianum
Campanula carpatica,
   isophylla, and other
   low-growing forms
Doronicum
Erythronium
Gentians (autumn-flowering)
Lettuce
Lilies
Lobelia (perennial)
Narcissus (including daffodils)
Parochetus communis
Primroses
Strawberries
Trillium
Tuberous begonias
Viola sororia

Adapted from *The Complete Shade Gardener*, 2nd edition, by George Schenk (Boston: Houghton Mifflin, 1985), p.63.

To Learn More About Slugs

BOOKS

Harper, Alice Bryant, *The Banana Slug* (Aptos, CA: Bay Leaves Press, 1988)

Kennedy, Des, *Living Things We Love to Hate: Facts, Fantasies, and Fallacies* (Vancouver, B.C.: Whitecap Books, 1992)

Kozloff, Eugene, *Plants and Animals of the Pacific Northwest* (Seattle: University of Washington Press, 1976)

Solem, Alan, *The Shell Makers: Introducing Mollusks* (New York: John Wiley & Sons, 1974)

South, A., *Terrestrial Slugs: Biology, Ecology, and Control* (London: Chapman & Hall, 1992)

ARTICLES

Branson, Branley A., "Collections of Gastropods from the Cascade Mountains of Washington," *The Veliger*, Vol. 23, No. 2

_____. "Freshwater and Terrestrial Mollusca of the Olympic Peninsula, Washington," *The Veliger*, Vol. 19, No. 3

Dickey, Philip, "The Baiting Game: Meeting Slimy Pests in the Garden," *Alternatives* (the quarterly newsletter of the Washington Toxics Coalition), Fall 1993

Gauger, Rick, "The Lives of a Slug," *Pacific Northwest*, Volume 17, No. 4, May 1983

Hanna, G. Dallas, "Introduced Mollusks of Western North America," *Occasional Papers of the California Academy of Sciences*, No. 48, February 1966

Rollo, C. David, and Wellington, William G., "Why Slugs Squabble," *Natural History*, November 1977